To Erbis W. Tennant
on her 100th birthday,
October 18, 2022.

Tea Cakes, Quilts, and Sonshine

Story © Christina E. Petrides
Illustrations and design © Nika Tchaikovskaya

Publisher: Tchaikovsky·Family·Books
Republic of Korea, Jeju Island
e-mail: tyfamilybooks@gmail.com
instagram: @jeju_draw

ISBN 979-11-966402-5-5
First Edition, 2022
Set in Alphabetized Cassette Tapes Regular - a typeface licensed for this print edition from Brittney Murphey Design

Christina E. Petrides

Tea Cakes,
Quilts,
and Sonshine

illustrated by Nika Tchaikovskaya

At least once a week, Mrs. Tennant made tea cakes.

She always used her mother's
old tea cake recipe:

"Mix the batter smooth.
Spoon onto pans.
Slide pans into oven.
Bake to crisp perfection."

At four o'clock each day,
Mrs. Tennant made a pot of coffee
and sat down with Mr. Tennant on their porch.

They read the mail, looked through the local paper, sipped their coffee, and nibbled tea cakes.

And whenever she had even
a few minutes of free time,

Mrs. Tennant worked on a quilt.

After cutting out

colorful rectangles,

squares, triangles, and circles,

she sewed the pieces together

into big squares

and ironed them smooth.

She laid out the squares on the clean den floor
to decide what order looked best
before she turned them into a quilt.

When he finished working outdoors in his blueberry patch,
Mr. Tennant sat on the den sofa and admired his wife's sewing.

"Every quilt should have a little red in it!" he always said.

And Mrs. Tennant agreed.

when life gives YOU SCRAPS make a QUILT

and all THE TREE in the FIELD will CLA THEIR HANDS

Each week, Mrs. Tennant set aside some time
for what she called a Sonshine Program.

Because she believed that Jesus, the Son of God,
loved her very much,
she wanted to share the love she felt
with people around her,

especially with the residents of her town's two nursing homes.

Mrs. Tennant's Sonshine Program became a huge success!

Residents of the nursing homes
eagerly awaited the arrival of the Tennants
and their young grandchildren.

Each Sonshine Program
began with a joke.

Or two.

Then Mrs. Tennant led the group in singing hymns and gave a short, simple devotional.

Sometimes, a guest would play the piano.

At the end of the program,
Mr. Tennant gave a small bag of tea cakes
to each person there.

Mrs. Tennant often brought in a quilt she was working on.

The old ladies and men loved seeing how it gradually took shape.

Until she was older than many people in the nursing homes,
Mrs. Tennant continued her Sonshine Programs.

Ultimately, Mrs. Tennant made more than one hundred quilts.

Most had a little red in them,

as Mr. Tennant had suggested.

And she baked thousands of tea cakes.

Her grandchildren still use that same old recipe.

Nowadays, when I sit on the porch nibbling a tea cake,
a quilt hugging my shoulders...

I think about the sweetness, warmth,

and Sonshine

that my Grandmommy, Mrs. Tennant,

has brought to countless people during her century-long life.

Dear Reader,

Tea Cakes, Quilts, and Sonshine

is a companion to my first children's book,

Blueberry Man.

While that was a true story about my grandfather, this is a true story about my grandmother, his wife.

Each of them had difficulties in their lives, but they used their God-given skills to bless others.

I hope that you will be encouraged by their example.

Christina E. Petrides

www.christinaepetrides.com